2116

How Big is Big?

HOT SCIENCE EXPERIMENTS

Science Projects with Volume

ROBERT GARDNER

ILLUSTRATED BY TOM LABAFF

Enslow Elementary

an imprint of

Enslow Publishers, Inc.

40 Industrial Road
Box 398
Berkeley Heights, NJ 07922
USA

http://www.enslow.com

Enslow Elementary, an imprint of Enslow Publishers, Inc.

Enslow Elementary® is a registered trademark of Enslow Publishers, Inc.

Originally published as *Super-Sized Science Projects with Volume: How Much Space Does It Take Up?* in 2003."

Library of Congress Cataloging-in-Publication Data

Gardner, Robert, 1929– author.
    [Super-sized science projects with volume]
    How big is big? : science projects with volume / Robert Gardner.
        pages cm. — (Hot science experiments)
    "Originally published as Super-Sized Science Projects with Volume: How Much Space Does It Take Up? in 2003."
    Audience: K to grade 3.
    Includes bibliographical references and index.
    ISBN 978-0-7660-6620-5
    1. Volume (Cubic content—Juvenile literature. 2. Science—Experiments—Juvenile literature.
3. Science projects—Juvenile literature. I. Title.
    QC104.G37 2015
    530.8'078—dc23
                        2014027427

Future editions:
Paperback ISBN: 978-0-7660-6621-2
EPUB ISBN: 978-0-7660-6622-9
Single-User PDF ISBN: 978-0-7660-6623-6
Multi-User PDF ISBN: 978-0-7660-6624-3

Printed in the United States of America
102014 Bang Printing, Brainerd, Minn.
10 9 8 7 6 5 4 3 2 1

To Our Readers: We have done our best to make sure all Internet Addresses in this book were active and appropriate when we went to press. However, the author and the publisher have no control over and assume no liability for the material available on those Internet sites or on other Web sites they may link to. Any comments or suggestions can be sent by e-mail to comments@enslow.com or to the address on the back cover.

♻ Enslow Publishers, Inc., is committed to printing our books on recycled paper. The paper in every book contains 10% to 30% post-consumer waste (PCW). The cover board on the outside of each book contains 100% PCW. Our goal is to do our part to help young people and the environment too!

Illustration Credits: Tom Labaff (tomlabaff.com)

Cover Credits: Tom Labaff (tomlabaff.com)

Contents

🎗 Contains ideas for science fair projects.

Measuring— How Big Is It?

As you grow, you take up more space. The shoes you buy one year may not fit you the next. Your feet grow and take up more space, so you have to buy bigger shoes.

The amount of space something takes up is called its volume. Volume can be found by taking measurements. To measure volume, you can use a ruler or tape measure, or you can use a measuring cup or graduated cylinder.

Many solids can be measured simply in three directions. Using a ruler or tape measure, you can find out how high, how long, and how wide they are. Multiplying these measurements will tell you each object's volume. For example, if you multiply the length of a box of tissues times its height, then times its width, you will know its cubic measure—its volume.

Objects that have an irregular shape, such as your thumb, can be measured by displacement. The object can be put into a measuring cup or graduated cylinder that contains some water.

The difference in water level will tell you the object's volume (although it won't tell you your glove size!). Fluids—liquids and gases—can also be measured by displacement.

In most countries, volume is measured in metric units, such as cubic meters, cubic centimeters or milliliters, and liters. In the United States, we use both metric units and U.S. customary units. U.S. customary units include the cubic inch, cubic foot, and cubic yard. Pints, quarts, and gallons are also used to measure volume. We buy milk in quart or gallon containers and water in ½-, 1-, and 3-liter bottles. You will learn about the units used to measure volume in the experiments in this book.

Measurement Abbreviations	
cm	centimeter
cc	cubic centimeter
ft	foot, feet
in	inch
L	liter
m	meter
mL	milliliter

Entering a Science Fair

Some of the experiments in this book might give you ideas for a science fair project. Those experiments are marked with a 🎖 symbol. Remember, judges at science fairs like experiments that are imaginative. It is hard to be creative if you are not interested in your project. Pick a subject that you enjoy and want to know more about.

You can add to the value of the experiments you do by keeping notes. Set up an experiment notebook and record your work carefully. As you do some of these experiments, you might think of new questions that you can answer with experiments of your own. Go ahead and carry out these experiments (with your parents' or teacher's permission). You are developing the kind of curiosity that is shared by all scientists.

If you enter a science fair, you should read some of the books listed in the back of this book. They will give you helpful hints and lots of useful information about science fairs. You will learn how to prepare great reports that include charts and graphs. You will also learn how to set up and display your work, how to present your project, and how to talk with judges and visitors.

Safety First

As you do the activities and experiments in this or any other book, do them safely. Remember the rules listed below and follow them closely.

1. Any experiments that you do should be done under the supervision of a parent, teacher, or another adult.

2. Read all instructions carefully. If you have questions, check with an adult. Do not take chances.

3. If you work with a friend who enjoys science too, keep a serious attitude while experimenting. Fooling around can be dangerous to you and to others.

4. Keep the area where you are experimenting clean and organized. When you have finished, clean up and put away the materials you were using.

Measuring with Cubes

A cube is an object whose length, width, and height are equal.

Let's Get Started!

1. Using modeling clay and a ruler, make a cube whose length, width, and height are all one centimeter (1 cm). The cube you have made has a volume of one cubic centimeter (1 cc).

2. Make 7 more cubes of one cubic centimeter from clay. Put these cubes together to make a cube that is 2 cm long, 2 cm wide, and 2 cm high. This larger cube is made of 8 smaller cubes, each with a volume of 1 cc. The volume of the larger cube, then, must be 8 cubic centimeters (8 cc).

3. Other than counting cubes, is there another way to find the volume of a solid object? Try this! Multiply the length times the width times the height. As you can see:

$$2 \text{ cm} \times 2 \text{ cm} \times 2 \text{ cm} = 8 \text{ cubic centimeters (cc)}$$
$$\text{length} \times \text{width} \times \text{height} = \text{volume}$$

4. Use the 8 cubes to build a solid 4 cm long, 2 cm wide, and 1 cm tall. What is its volume? To find out, multiply its length times width times height.

5. With the same 8 cubes, build a solid 8 cm long, 1 cm wide, and 1 cm high. What is its volume? (Save the clay cubes for future experiments.)

6. Using what you have learned, find the volume of some regular solid objects such as blocks and boxes.

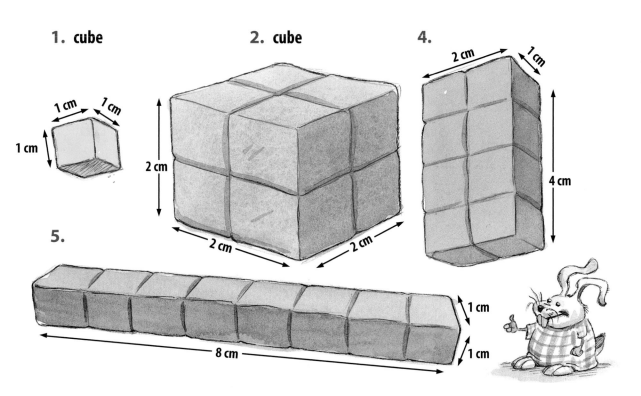

1. **cube**

1 cm 1 cm 1 cm

2. **cube**

2 cm 2 cm 2 cm

4.

2 cm 1 cm 4 cm

5.

8 cm 1 cm 1 cm

Cubic Friends

Volume is easily measured in cubic centimeters, but it can be measured in other units as well. In the metric system, large volumes are often measured in cubic meters.

Let's Get Started!

WHAT YOU NEED:

- meterstick
- chalk or stick to draw with
- 4 friends
- 4 sticks each cut to 1 meter long

1. To get a feeling for the volume of a cubic meter, draw a square one meter on each side on the ground or pavement.

2. Have each of four friends stand at the corners of the square. Measure up one meter from the ground. Ask each friend to hold the ends of two 1-meter-long sticks horizontally at that height, as shown in the drawing.

The sticks form the top of a cubic meter. The space between the square on the ground and the square made by the four horizontal sticks is a cubic meter. Could you fit inside a cubic meter?

Why is it better to use cubic meters than cubic centimeters to measure the volume of large spaces or objects?

Ideas for Your Science Fair

Using a meterstick or metric tape measure, find the length, width, and height of your classroom. What is the volume of your classroom in cubic meters? What is the volume of your bedroom?

The volume of an ocean is usually measured in cubic kilometers. What is a cubic kilometer?

Inch, Foot, and Yard

The U.S. customary measurements of solid objects are based on the inch, foot, and yard.

Let's Get Started!

1. Take some modeling clay and make a solid cube that is 1 inch long, 1 inch wide, and 1 inch high. You have made a cubic inch. Is it larger or smaller than the cubic centimeter you made in the first experiment? About how many times larger or smaller?

2. One foot is 12 inches long. Using cardboard, scissors, and tape, build a cubic box that has a volume of 1 cubic foot. How many cubic inches are in 1 cubic foot? Remember, there are 12 inches in a foot. Multiply the height (12 inches) by the width (12 inches) by the depth (12 inches). How many cubic inches are in 2 cubic feet? In 10 cubic feet? (See answers on page 47.)

3. One yard is 3 feet long. Therefore, a cubic yard is 3 feet long, 3 feet wide, and 3 feet high. Together with some friends, use cardboard, scissors, and tape to build a cubic box that contains 1 cubic yard. Remember how you figured out the cubic inches in a cubic foot. How many cubic feet are in a cubic yard? In 3 cubic yards? In 10 cubic yards? (See answers on page 47.)

4. Sand and gravel are sold by the cubic yard. Suppose a homeowner has a large hole in her lawn that is 12 feet long, 9 feet wide, and 6 feet deep. She wants to fill the hole with gravel. How many cubic yards of gravel should she have delivered to fill the hole? (See answer on page 47.)

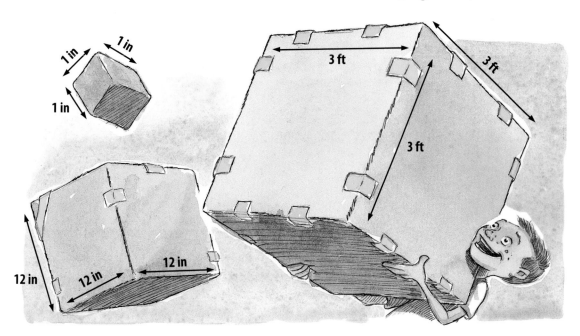

Cup, Pint, Quart, and Gallon

You have used cubic inches, cubic feet, and cubic yards to measure the volume of solids. Different units are usually used to measure the volume of liquids. In this experiment, you will use the U.S. customary units of cups, pints, quarts, and gallons to measure liquid volumes. Record all your results in a notebook.

Let's Get Started!

1. Find a measuring cup and pint, quart, and gallon containers. Look closely at the measuring cup. How many ounces are equal to 1 cup?

2. Fill the measuring cup to the 1-cup level with water. Pour the water into the pint container. Continue to fill the pint container with cups of water. How many cups does it take to fill the pint container?

3. Fill the quart container with cups of water. How many cups does it take to fill the quart container?

4. Now use the quart container to fill the gallon container. How many quarts are equal to 1 gallon?

From the results of the experiment you have just done, answer the following questions.

How many pints of water are needed to fill a 1-gallon container?

How many cups of water are needed to fill a 1-gallon container?

How many ounces of water are needed to fill a 1-gallon container?

How many ounces of water are in 1 quart of water?

Liter vs. Quart and Milliliter

If you drink soda or bottled water, you know that liquid volumes can be measured in liters.

Let's Get Started!

1. To see how a liter compares with a quart, fill an empty 1-liter (1-L) bottle with water. Then pour that water into a quart container. Is a liter greater or smaller than a quart? About how much more or less?

2. Look closely at a metric measuring cup. The prefix *milli* as seen in *milliliter* (mL) means "one-thousandth" (1/1000 or .001). Fill a metric measuring cup to the 250-milliliter (mL) line with water. Pour that water into an empty 1-L container. How many times do you have to pour 250 mL into the 1-L container to fill it? How many milliliters are equal to 1 liter?

3. Find a 100-mL graduated cylinder. (Your school's science teacher can probably help you.) How many times do you think you will have to use the 100-mL cylinder to fill a 1-L container? Try it. Was your prediction correct?

4. How many times will you have to fill the 100-mL graduated cylinder in order to fill the metric measuring cup to the 250-mL line?

How does this experiment demonstrate that *milli-* means "one-thousandth"?

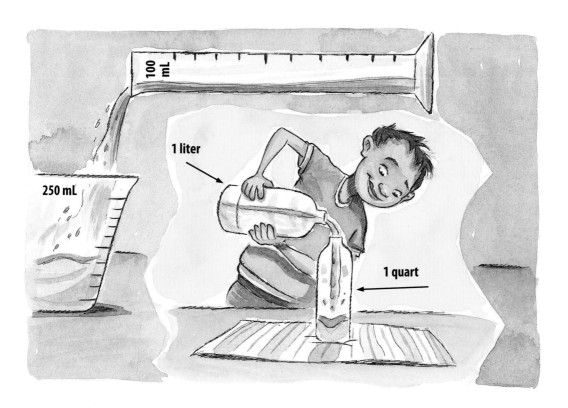

Volume of a Drop

A drop of water has a very small volume, but you can find out what it is. All you need is a little patience.

WHAT YOU NEED:

- drinking glass
- water
- eyedropper
- medicine cup that measures volume in milliliters (mL) or cubic centimeters (cc)
- calculator

Let's Get Started!

1. Fill the glass with water. Squeeze the eyedropper bulb to remove some water from the glass. Release water one drop at a time from the dropper.

2. Get the metric medicine cup. It makes no difference which units are on the cup. A milliliter is equal to a cubic centimeter.

3. Use the dropper to add water drop by drop to the cup. Count the drops until you have 10 mL (10 cc) of water. If it takes 200 drops to fill the cup to the 10 mL line, the volume of one drop must be

$$10 \text{ mL} \div 200 \text{ drops} = 10/200$$
$$= 1/20 \text{ or } .05 \text{ mL}$$

What is the volume of one drop of water according to your measurements? Use a calculator to do the arithmetic.

Ideas for Your Science Fair

Does a drop of hot tap water have the same volume as a drop of cold tap water? Does a drop of rubbing alcohol have the same volume as a drop of water? How about a drop of soapy water? Design your own experiments to answer these questions.

Air Takes Up Space

Air occupies space. You can see that this is true.

Let's Get Started!

1. Find a plastic jar or bottle that has a narrow neck and mouth. Put the spout of a plastic funnel into the neck of the plastic jar or bottle.

2. Add a few drops of food coloring to some water in a small container. Pour some of the colored water into the funnel. You can see that the water flows into the jar.

3. Next, use some modeling clay to seal the space between the funnel's spout and the mouth of the bottle, as shown in the drawing. When the bottle is sealed, pour more colored water into the funnel.

   This time the water stays in the funnel. Very little water flows into the jar or bottle. Why?

WHAT YOU NEED:
- plastic jar or bottle with a narrow neck and mouth
- plastic funnel
- food coloring
- water
- small container
- modeling clay

Since the bottle is sealed, water cannot push air out of the bottle. Air cannot get out of the bottle because the mouth of the bottle has been sealed.

What do you think will happen to the water in the funnel if you remove some clay so that the neck is no longer sealed? Try it! Was your prediction correct?

Underwater Mystery

Here is another way to show that air takes up space.

Let's Get Started!

WHAT YOU NEED:

- plastic jar
- water
- large pan
- measuring cup with metric units
- the 8 cubic centimeters of clay made in the first experiment

1. Fill a plastic jar about halfway with water. Also, nearly fill a large pan with water. Put your hand over the mouth of the jar. Turn the jar upside down and put it in the pan. The jar's mouth should be under the water in the pan. Remove your hand. Where is the air in the jar now?

2. Keeping the jar's mouth under water, move the bottle up and down. Does the air stay in the bottle?

3. Slowly turn the bottle on its side. More water can now enter the jar. How can you tell that air is being pushed out of the bottle? What is now taking up the space that was occupied by the air?

You have just seen that water can fill the space taken up by air. Can a solid replace the volume occupied by a liquid? Try the next experiment to find out.

Displacing Water

Two things cannot occupy the same space. In the case of water and air, water will push air out of the space it occupies. In the same way, a solid will displace a volume of water equal to its own volume. Prove this with the following simple experiment.

Let's Get Started!

1. Using modeling clay, make a solid that has a volume of 50 cubic centimeters. A solid 5 cm x 5 cm x 2 cm will work nicely. Since a cubic centimeter and a milliliter have the same volume, the solid should displace 50 mL of water.

2. Fill a metric measuring cup to the 200-mL line. Then carefully put the solid piece of clay into the water. What is the volume now, according to the water level in the measuring cup? How can you tell that a solid displaces its own volume of water?

3. If you change the clay's shape into a ball, will its volume change? Design an experiment to find out.

Ideas for Your Science Fair

Use water and a measuring cup or graduated cylinder to find the volume of things whose dimensions are not easily measured. You might try stones, marbles, erasers, pencils, coins, and other objects that will fit into the cup or cylinder. Remember, for identical objects, you can use more than one if the volume of one is too small to measure accurately.

Seeds and Water

Before seeds sprout, they take in water. You can measure the volume of water a seed takes in.

Let's Get Started!

1. Put 50 mL of water in a 100-mL metric measuring cup or graduated cylinder. Put 10 lima bean seeds into the water. What is the water level after the seeds are added? What is the volume of the seeds? What is the average volume of one lima bean seed?

2. Put the seeds in a quart container, cover them with water, and leave them overnight. The next day, remove the seeds from the water. Dry them gently with paper towels and gently put them back in a 100-mL graduated cylinder with

50 mL of water. What is their volume now? How many milliliters of water did the bean seeds absorb? What is the average volume of a lima bean seed now? What was the average amount of water absorbed by each lima bean seed?

Idea for Your Science Fair

How does the average volume of water taken up by a lima bean seed compare with the volume of water taken up by other seeds? You might try seeds of other beans, as well as corn kernels, peas, squash seeds, pumpkin seeds, and other kinds of seeds.

How Much Air Is in Sand?

WHAT YOU NEED:
- dry sand
- graduated cylinder
- notebook and pencil
- container to hold sand
- water
- sheet of paper

Let's Get Started!

1. Pour dry sand into a graduated cylinder until it is about half full. Write down the sand's volume. Sand is made up of small grains with air between them. The volume you measured is actually the volume of the sand and the air between the sand grains. Find the volume of the sand alone.

28

2. Pour the sand you measured into a separate container. Add water to the graduated cylinder until it is about half full. Write down this volume.

Data Table	
1. Volume of dry sand and air	50 mL
2. Volume of water	50 mL
3. Volume of sand and water	80 mL

3. Use a folded sheet of paper to carefully pour the sand you measured into the water. Water will take the place of the air in the sand. Write down the volume of the sand and water.

4. What is the volume of the dry sand and air? What is the volume of the water alone? What is the volume of the sand and water? What is the volume of sand alone? What fraction of the dry sand is air?

Suppose your results look like those in the data table shown. The volume of the sand alone would be:

sand and water − water = sand alone (80 mL − 50 mL = 30 mL)

The air in the sand would be:

dry sand − sand alone = air in sand (50 mL − 30 mL = 20 mL)

So the fraction of the dry sand that is air would be:

air ÷ dry sand = percentage of sand that is air
(20 mL ÷ 50 mL = 20/50
= 2/5 or .40 or 40 percent)

- ball of steel wool (do not use soap–filled steel wool pads)
- vinegar
- bowl
- shallow pan
- food coloring
- ruler
- water
- sink
- tall, narrow jar, such as an olive jar, or large test tube
- pencil
- marking pen or rubber band

What Fraction of Air Is Oxygen?

Air is made up of mostly oxygen and nitrogen, two gases without smell or color. You can find out what fraction of air is oxygen.

Let's Get Started!

1. Remove a few strands from a large ball of steel wool. (Do not use soap-filled steel wool pads.) Roll them into a loosely packed ball and soak it in a bowl of vinegar for about an hour.

2. While the steel wool is soaking, fill a shallow pan to a depth of about 2 cm (1 in) with colored water.

3. Shake the vinegar from the steel wool into a sink. Then put the ball of steel wool into a tall narrow jar. Use a pencil to push the ball all the way to the bottom of the jar. Turn the jar upside down and place it in the pan of water. If necessary, fasten the jar so that it won't tip over.

The steel will react with oxygen, removing it from the air trapped in the jar. The remaining gas in the jar will be mostly nitrogen.

4. After 24 hours, mark the water level in the jar with a marking pen or rubber band. Leave the jar for several hours. Once the water level has stopped rising, look closely at the steel wool in the jar. What has the oxygen done to it?

Use a ruler to measure the height of the water that replaced the oxygen in the jar (A). Also measure the total inside height of the jar (B). The fraction of air that is oxygen is:

$$\text{Fraction of air that is oxygen} = \frac{(A)}{(B)}$$

What fraction of the air is oxygen according to your measurements?

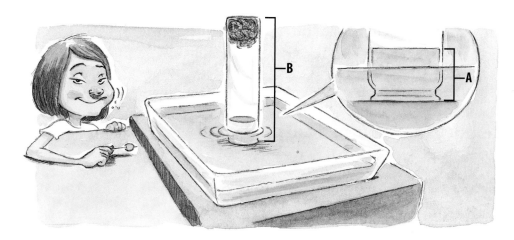

Temperature and the Volume of a Gas

WHAT YOU NEED:
- balloon
- narrow–necked 1½– or 2–liter plastic soda bottle
- pail
- hot and cold tap water
- refrigerator
- freezer
- clock or watch

Let's Get Started!

1. Pull the neck of an empty balloon over the mouth of a large, empty, narrow-necked plastic soda bottle. Hold the bottle in a pail of hot tap water. What happens to the balloon? What went into the balloon? What happens to the volume of a gas, such as the air in the bottle, when its temperature rises?

2. Remove the bottle from the hot water. Let it cool for a few minutes. What happens to the volume of the gas in the balloon and bottle as they cool?

3. Remove the balloon. Rinse the bottle several times with hot water. The warm bottle will heat air entering the bottle after the water is poured out. Put the empty balloon back on the

soda bottle. What happens to the balloon as the air inside the bottle cools?

4. To further lower the temperature of the air, put the bottle in a refrigerator. After a few minutes, open the refrigerator. What happened to the balloon as the air in the bottle grew colder?

5. To cool the air even more, put the bottle in a freezer, where the temperature is very cold. After about 10 minutes, remove the bottle. What has happened to the volume of the air in the bottle and balloon when the temperature cooled.

6. Remove the bottle from the freezer. What do you think will happen as the temperature of the air in the bottle and balloon rises to room temperature? Were you right?

Ideas for Your Science Fair

Based on what you have learned in this experiment, make a gas thermometer.

Do all gases expand and contract with temperature in the same way?

Temperature and the Volume of a Liquid

Does the volume of a liquid change when its temperature changes?

Let's Get Started!

1. Fill a test tube or similar tube to the top with colored water. Find a one-hole rubber stopper that fits the test tube. If you do not have a rubber stopper, use clay to make a plug for the test tube.

2. Coat the outside of one end of a clear plastic drinking straw with petroleum jelly. Push this end of the straw through the hole in the rubber stopper. If you are using a clay plug, make a hole in it with a pencil. Push the straw through the hole in the clay. The straw should fit tightly.

3. Insert the rubber stopper or clay plug firmly into the mouth of the tube. The water level should rise about halfway up the drinking straw and stay there.

4. Place the test tube in a glass. Let it stand for 10 minutes. Then mark the water level on the straw with a marking pen.

5. Put the test tube in a container filled with hot water. What happens to the water level in the straw?

6. Next, put the tube in a container filled with cold water. What happens to the water level in the straw? What happens to the volume of water when its temperature rises? What happens to the volume of water when its temperature falls?

Freezing and the Volume of Water

In the previous experiment, you saw that the volume of water shrinks when it grows colder. But what happens when liquid water freezes and becomes solid water (ice)?

Let's Get Started!

1. Place a clear plastic drinking straw in a tall glass of water. Put the tip of your index finger firmly over the top of the straw as shown. You can now lift the straw out of the glass, and water will stay in the straw.

2. Keep your finger on the straw as you seal the lower end of the straw by pushing it gently into a lump of modeling clay. You can now remove your finger. The water should remain in the straw.

3. Use a marking pen to carefully and gently mark the water level on the straw. Lift the clay with the water-filled straw and place it upright in a freezer. Leave the water-filled straw in the freezer for about an hour or so. Then look at the level of the ice in the straw. What happens to the volume of water when it turns to solid ice?

4. What do you think the volume will be after the solid water melts back to liquid water? After the ice has melted, examine the water level in the straw. Were you correct?

Ideas for Your Science Fair

By what fraction of its volume does water expand when it freezes? In what ways is water an unusual liquid?

The Volume of a Breath

How deep a breath do you take?

WHAT YOU NEED:

- clear, empty, rigid container big enough to hold your fist
- masking tape
- pen or marker
- metric measuring cup or graduated cylinder
- plastic bag about 15 cm x 20 cm (6 in x 8 in)
- twistie
- notebook and pencil

Let's Get Started!

1. Find a clear, empty, rigid container big enough to hold your fist. A large, wide-mouth jar will do. Apply a piece of masking tape to its side from bottom to top. Using a measuring cup, pour 100 mL of water into the container. Make a mark on the tape indicating the water level in the container. Label it 100 mL. Continue adding water, 100 mL at a time, and marking the depth until the container is nearly full.

2. Begin your experiment with the container about half full. Squeeze any air from a plastic bag about 15 cm x 20 cm (6 in x 8 in). **Never put a plastic bag over your head!** While breathing at your normal rate, hold your nose so that

all the air passes through your mouth. After breathing this way for several minutes, place the open end of the plastic bag firmly around your mouth just before you exhale. Collect the exhaled air in the bag. Seal off the bag with a twistie. The bag contains the air you exhaled.

3. To find the volume you exhaled, hold the air-filled bag in your hand and push your hand under the water. Record the new water level in the container. Mark your wrist where it touches the water. Remove your hand from the water. Squeeze all the air out of the bag. Hold it in your fist and push your hand into the water to the mark on your wrist. Again, record the water level. Use the data from your experiment to find out how much air you breathe in one breath.

Volume of one breath = (water level with hand and air-filled bag) − (water level with empty bag and hand)

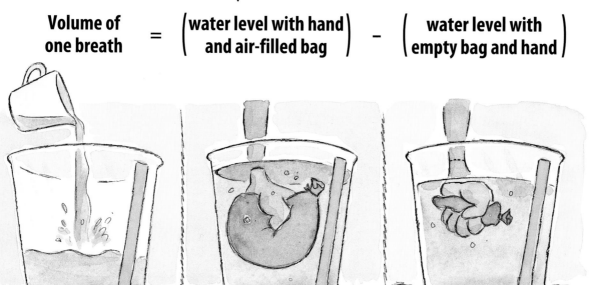

Volume of a Deep Breath

In the previous experiment you measured the volume of air you exhale in a single normal breath. But suppose you take a deep breath. Great swimmers and divers can take very deep breaths. How much air can you exhale after taking a deep breath?

WHAT YOU NEED:
- 1–gallon plastic milk container
- water
- large pan
- rubber or plastic tube about 45 cm (18 in) long
- a friend
- marking pen

Let's Get Started!

1. Fill a 1-gallon plastic milk container with water. Put the cap on, and turn the water-filled container upside down in a pan of water.

2. Remove the cap underwater. Put one end of some rubber or plastic tubing into the mouth of the container as shown. Have a friend tip the container a little so that it does not squeeze the tubing.

3. Take a deep breath, then exhale as much air as you can through the tube into the water-filled jug. The air you exhale will replace

some of the water in the container. As soon as you have exhaled as much air as possible, squeeze the end of the tube near your mouth and remove the tube from the container. Mark the water level on the container with a marking pen.

4. Empty any remaining water from the container. Then use a metric measuring cup to find the volume of water needed to fill the container to the mark you made. How much air did you exhale? In the previous experiment you found out how much air you normally exhale. How many times as much air did you exhale after taking a deep breath?

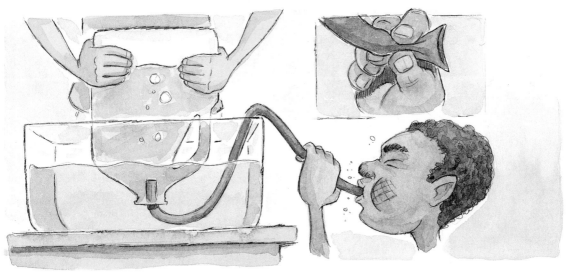

....
Idea for Your Science Fair
Investigate the meaning of the following terms: *vital capacity, tidal air, complemental air, supplemental air,* and *residual air.*

Testing Paper Towels

Do some brands of paper towels really absorb more water than others? Or do all paper towels absorb about the same amount of water?

Let's Get Started!

1. Fill a metric measuring cup to the 250-mL line with water. Take a paper towel and fold it so that it will fit into the cup. Then submerge it in the cup for a few seconds.

2. Remove the towel. Let excess water drip back into the cup. Don't squeeze the towel. How much water remains in the cup? How much water did the towel absorb? Write down the volume absorbed and the paper towel brand.

3. Repeat the experiment using different paper towel brands. Are all the brands the same? If not, which brand do you find absorbs the most water?

4. Check the label of each brand you tested. How many towels are on each roll of the brands you tested? Which brand absorbs the most water per roll? Is it the same brand as the single towel that absorbs the most water?

Ideas for Your Science Fair

What was the cost of a roll of each brand you tested? Which brand absorbs the most water per penny spent?

Would you advise people to buy a certain brand of paper towel? If so, what brand would you recommend? Why?

For each brand you tested, how much water, in grams, was absorbed per gram of dry towel?

Words to Know

cube—A solid whose length, width, and height are equal.

cubic—Describes a volume equal to a space that is 1 unit wide, 1 equal unit long, and 1 equal unit high. The unit may be any measure of length, such as a foot, inch, meter, or yard.

cubic centimeter—A volume equal to a space that is 1 centimeter long, 1 centimeter wide, and 1 centimeter high. A cubic centimeter has the same volume as a milliliter. The volume of objects of any shape can be measured in cubic centimeters.

cubic foot—A volume equal to a space that is 1 foot long, wide, and high.

cubic inch—A volume equal to a space that is 1 inch long, wide, and high.

cubic meter—A volume equal to a space that is 1 meter long, wide, and high.

cubic yard—A volume equal to a space that is 1 yard long, wide, and high.

dimension—The length, width, or height of an object.

displace—To push something out of the way. Water can displace air; solids can displace water.

exhale—The part of breathing during which air is forced out of the lungs.

fluid—Any substance that flows, such as a liquid or gas.

freezing—The changing of a liquid to a solid when the temperature decreases.

graduated cylinder—A calibrated container used to measure volumes of fluids or of solids by displacement.

inhale—The part of breathing during which air is drawn into the lungs.

liter—A volume equal to 1,000 cubic centimeters, 1,000 milliliters, or $\frac{1}{1,000}$ of a cubic meter.

measuring cup—A calibrated cup used to measure volumes of fluids or of solids by displacement.

melting—The changing of a solid to a liquid when the temperature rises.

oxygen—One of the gases that makes up air. It is the gas needed for most animals to live.

volume—The space taken up by an object or substance.

Further Reading

Benhoff, Susan. *Measurement.* Greensboro, N.C.: Carson-Dellosa Publishing Company, Inc., 1998.

Henderson, Joyce and Heather Tomasello. *So You Have to Do a Science Fair Project.* New York: Wiley, 2006.

Kensler, Chris. *Secret Treasures and Magical Measures: Adventures in Measuring: Time, Temperature, Length, Weight, Volume, Angles, Shapes and Money.* New York: Simon & Schuster, 2003.

Somervill Barbara A. *Measure It!: Distance, Area, and Volume.* North Mankato, Minn.: Heinemann InfoSearch/Capstone, 2010.

VanCleave, Janice. *VanCleave's Great Science Project Ideas from Real Kids.* New York: Wiley, 2006.

Walpole, Brenda. *Measuring Up with Science: Size.* Milwaukee: Gareth Stevens, 1995.

Westphal, Laurie. *Science Dictionary for Kids: The Essential Guide to Science Terms, Concepts, and Strategies.* Waco, Tex.: Prufrock Press , 2009.

Woodford, Chris. *Measure Up Math: Volume.* Milwaukee: Gareth Stevens Publishing, 2012.

Answers

p. 12   1 cubic foot = 1,728 cubic inches;
2 cubic feet = 3,456 cubic inches;
10 cubic feet = 17,280 cubic inches.

p. 13(a)   1 cubic yard = 27 cubic feet;
3 cubic yards = 81 cubic feet;
10 cubic yards = 270 cubic feet.

(b)   She will need 24 cubic yards of gravel
(12 feet x 9 feet x 6 feet = 4 yd x 3 yd x 2 yd = 24 cubic yards).

Index